A Miscellany of
WOMEN'S WISDOM

A Miscellany of

WOMEN'S
WISDOM

Jane Lyle

RUNNING PRESS
Philadelphia, Pennsylvania

Canadian representatives: General Publishing Co., Ltd.,
30 Lesmill Road, Don Mills, Ontario M3B 2T6.
International representatives: Worldwide Media Services, Inc.,
30 Montgomery Street, Jersey City, New Jersey 07302.

9 8 7 6 5 4 3 2 1
Digit on the right indicates the number of this printing.

Library of Congress Catalog Number 93-83522

ISBN 1-56138-313-9

A Miscellany of Women's Wisdom
Compiled by Jane Lyle
Edited by Diana Craig
Designed by Simon Jennings
Illustrations & engravings enhanced by Robin Harris

Produced, edited, and designed by Inklink,
Greenwich, London, England
Published in the United States by Running Press,
Philadelphia, Pennsylvania
Typeset in Garamond by Inklink
Printed in Hong Kong by South Sea International Press

This book may be ordered by mail from the publisher.
Please add $2.50 for postage and handling.
But try your bookstore first!
Running Press Book Publishers
125 South Twenty-Second Street
Philadelphia, Pennsylvania 19103

A MISCELLANY OF

WOMEN'S WISDOM

TABLE OF

CONTENTS

ARRANGED IN SIX CHAPTERS

"There is a woman at the beginning of all great things."

ALPHONSE DE LAMARTINE (1790-1869)

I GREW UP TAKING A LOT FOR GRANTED: *I expected to vote, to be able to borrow money, to be taken seriously, and to be free to travel wherever and whenever I wanted. It was a long time before I realized that women in other times had had to fight for these privileges, as a knowledge of the shape and texture of women's lives did not form the greater part of my historical education. In an attempt to learn more about women's lives – both in general and in the minutest domestic detail – I eagerly read whatever I could find, from the yellowing pages of Victorian women's magazines to scholarly studies of women in the ancient world. I became fascinated by mythology, in which women invariably played such a crucial part as powerful goddesses.*

Researching this book has, therefore, been a personal voyage of discovery and inspiration. Much has changed, but in essence women are the same as they have always been. A harassed mother in ancient Greece, a Victorian artist, a Japanese courtesan, and a twentieth-century politician would all understand one another very well if they met, for they are women first and foremost, and share humanity's timeless concerns.

The miscellany presented here is, necessarily, idiosyncratic. It represents a small selection from a vast resource. Above all, it is a celebration of diversity. The wit, honesty, and spirit of the women who speak to us through these pages constitute, most assuredly, wisdom from which we can all benefit.

Jane Lyle

JANE LYLE

DEDICATED TO
WOMEN EVERYWHERE.
LET WISDOM PREVAIL.

CHAPTER ONE

WISE WOMEN

*"The entire being of a woman is a secret
which should be kept."*

From "OF HIDDEN THOUGHTS AND OF HEAVEN"
by ISAK DINESEN (BARONESS KAREN BLIXEN), 1957

*THE ENDURING FEMININE CONCERNS OF CONCEPTION,
PREGNANCY, AND BIRTH FORM THE CORNERSTONE OF A GREAT
STOREHOUSE OF SOUND COMMON SENSE, MYSTERY, AND MAGIC.
WHILE SOME TRADITIONAL REMEDIES ARE CLEARLY FOUNDED ON
SUPERSTITION, OTHERS CONTAIN FAMILIAR INGREDIENTS, AS
EFFECTIVE TODAY
AS THEY WERE CENTURIES AGO.*

A SACRED OATH

When doctors all over the world honor their entry into the medical profession by taking the Hippocratic Oath, they are duly acknowledging women's contribution to medicine. The Oath begins, "I swear by Apollo the physician, by Aesculapius, Hygeia and Panacea..." The two latter names were those of the daughters of Aesculapius, the mythic Greek god of medicine. Their names also live on in the words "hygiene" and "panacea," or cure-all, although Aesculapius' supportive wife, Epione, seems sadly to have been forgotten. In ancient Greece his whole family was highly regarded, and was honored in a multitude of shrines and temples dedicated to healing. Around three hundred have been discovered to date.

HELEN'S HERBS

Women's knowledge and use of herbs was relatively extensive in the ancient world. In his epic poem the *Odyssey*, Homer relates how Helen of Troy, legendary beauty of Greek myth, "cast a drug into the wine...a drug to lull all pain and anger, and bring forgetfulness of every sorrow." This was nepenthe, famed drug of the ancients. No one knows for certain what it contained, although suggestions include datura, poppy, borage, and verbena.

The herb elecampane (*Inula helenium*) is named after Helen of Troy. The plant is said to have sprung up from the ground where her tears fell while she was being abducted by Paris, clutching an abundant bunch of its bright yellow flowers. Traditionally, it was used to cure coughs, catarrh and overeating.

SOOTHING SORE THROATS

Cough syrups to soothe a sore throat are not a modern invention. Octavia, first wife of the Roman politician and soldier Mark Antony, created her own cough linctus. The recipe contains some familiar ingredients: honey, myrrh, caraway, celery, saffron, and anise.

MAGICAL MEDICINE

Healing and pain relief have always been regarded as sacred, magical activities – so it is not surprising that in the Middle Ages women healers were frequently believed to be witches because of their superior know-ledge of herbs. Among the Latin words for "witch" were *herberia* (one who gathers herbs), *veneficia* (poisoner), and *pixidria* (keeper of an ointment box).

OLD WIVES

"Are not philosophers, mathematicians and astrologers often inferior to country women in their divinations and predictions, and does not the old nurse very often beat the doctor?"
CORNELIUS AGRIPPA VON NETTESHEIM (c.1486-1535)

When doctors were few in number, and prohibitively expensive for ordinary people, everyone turned to "old wives" to cure their maladies. Some of their remedies – such as foxglove tea for heart conditions, or decoctions of willow bark to ease pain – remain the basis of widely used modern drugs such as aspirin.

WART CHARMING

Warts are unsightly, albeit harmless, afflictions. Getting rid of them has long been the province of witches and wart-charmers – generally women. The philosopher and essayist Francis Bacon (1561-1626) reported his own fascinating experience of this ancient practice:

"I had from my childhood a wart upon one of my fingers; afterwards, when I was about sixteen years old, being then at Paris, there grew upon both my hands a number of warts… in a month's space; the English Ambassador's lady, who was a woman far from superstition, told me one day she would help me away with my warts; whereupon she took a piece of lard with the skin on, and rubbed the warts all over… then she nailed the piece of lard with the fat toward the sun… The success was [such] that within five weeks' space all the warts went quite away…"

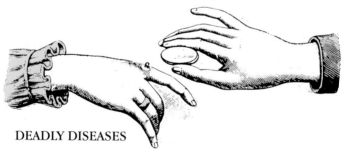

DEADLY DISEASES

The traditional remedies used by the "old wives" were not limited merely to the treatment of everyday complaints: they could also provide effective weapons against life-threatening illnesses.

CURING MALARIA

The Countess of Chinchon was the wife of the Spanish viceroy in seventeenth-century Peru. When she fell ill with malaria, she was cured by a preparation made from the bark of a tree – which was then named cinchona bark after her. She took the bark home to Spain, where many suffered from malaria, and thus brought this important substance to Europe. Cinchona bark yields quinine, a powerful antimalarial alkaloid.

PREVENTING SMALLPOX

Vaccination against the deadly disease of smallpox was practiced by Turkish women long before Edward Jenner (1749-1823) introduced it to an awestruck Europe in 1789. Lady Mary Montagu, an early feminist, observed it first-hand:

"There is a set of old women who make it their business to perform the operation every autumn in the month of September when the great heat is abated ... They make parties for the purpose ... The old woman comes with a nut-shell full of the matter of the best sort of smallpox, and asks what veins you please to have opened. She immediately rips open that you offer her, with a large needle (which gives you no more pain than a common scratch) and puts into the vein, as much matter as can lie upon the head of her needle, and after that binds up the little wound with a hollow bit of shell; and in this manner opens four or five veins."

From THE LETTERS OF THE RIGHT HONOURABLE
LADY MARY WORTLEY MONTAGU, 1717

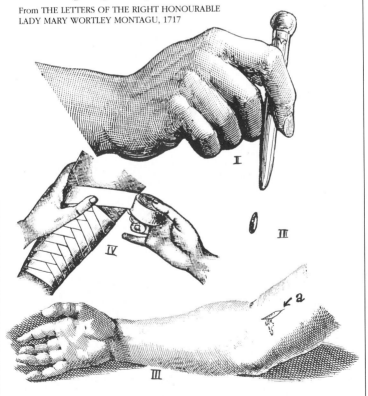

A QUEEN'S REMEDY

"Queen Elizabeth her potion for wind. Take ginger, cinnamon, galingale, of each one ounce; aniseeds, caraway seeds, fennel seeds, of each half an ounce; mace and nutmegs two drams each; pound all together and add one pound of white sugar. Use this powder after or before meat at any time. It comforteth the stomach, helpeth digestion, and expels wind greatly."

From THE FAIRFAX HOUSEHOLD BOOK
(SEVENTEENTH TO EIGHTEENTH CENTURY)

GALINGALE A medicinal herb.

BIRTH CONTROL

For thousands of years, women have sought to prevent conception and limit the number of children they produce. Many of their practices were probably ineffectual, and sometimes highly dangerous. Others were primitive versions of modern barrier methods.

One of the more alarming remedies was suggested by Aspasia, a Roman woman, in the second century A.D. She recommended a potentially poisonous drink made of absinthe, ox gall (bile from the gall bladder of an ox), and the herbs artemisia, eleterium, and rue.

Japanese women fared no better: they were offered a scalding hot contraceptive pulp of mercury, a leech, and a horsefly to drink. Their alternative was equally unappealing: "turnips in large quantities" with "monkey's brains in cold water," plus silver mercury scraped from the back of a mirror.

"Dr. Oster Mann recommends his Soluble Quinine Pessaries, which are at once harmless and effectual in preventing conception. The use of these Soluble Pessaries is not at all repulsive to the most refined and delicate feelings, and they possess distinct advantages when compared with other preventative checks."

From BIRTH CONTROL: HUSBAND AND WIFE'S HANDBOOK
by DR. OSTER MANN, 1930

PREGNANCY

"And so, to assist women, I intend to write of how to help their secret maladies so that one woman may aid another in her illness and not divulge her secrets to such discourteous men."
From THE SLOANE MANUSCRIPT, c.1450

The miracle of generation inspired awe in the ancient world, and dogma and heated controversy in the centuries that followed. It remains an area where women's instinctive knowledge emerges triumphant:

"For like as women take a greater pride in their beauty than pleasure or content in their virtue, so they take more pride in being with child than in having a child."
MARGARET CAVENDISH (1623-73)

"To me it is often a source of great pleasure and wonderment to see that the entire female body was created for the purpose of nurturing children."
MARTIN LUTHER (1483-1546)

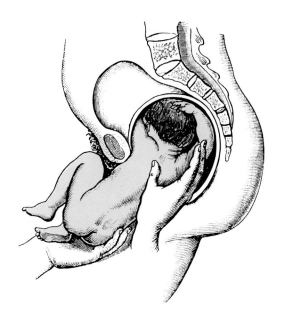

MIDWIVES

The title "midwife" is derived from the Anglo-Saxon word *med-wyf* – meaning "wise woman."

ROMAN MIDWIVES

In Ancient Rome, there were three kinds of official midwife. A woman who delivered babies was called an *obstetrix*; one who helped the new mother to breastfeed was known as a *nutrix*, or "nurturer"; while the religious and ritual elements of birth were the province of the *ceraria*, a priestess of the great mother goddess Ceres.

THE PERFECT MIDWIFE

Soranus, a Roman doctor practicing in the second century A.D., wrote this character study of the ideal midwife:

"She will be unperturbed, unafraid in danger, able to state clearly the reasons for her measures, she will bring reassurance to her patients, and be sympathetic. She must love work in order to persevere through all vicissitudes (for a woman who wishes to acquire such vast knowledge needs manly patience)."

WICKED WITCHES

After the decline of ancient Rome, the status of the midwife plummeted. For many dark and dismal centuries midwives and witches were considered to be one and the same – heretical and dangerous. In England in 1559, the Parliamentary Articles of Enquiry urged churchmen to be vigilant in matters of "charms, sorcery, enchantments, invocations, circles, witchcrafts, soothsaying…especially in the time of women's travails."

"No one does more harm to the Catholic faith than midwives."
From MALLEUS MALEFICARUM ("THE HAMMER OF EVILDOERS"), 1484

PRENATAL CARE

To avoid a miscarriage, Roman women were advised to eschew worrying, vigorous exercise and chariot rides.

"It is better and more seemly that a wise woman learned in the art should visit a sick woman and inquire into the secrets of her nature and her hidden parts, than that a man should do so, for whom it is not lawful to see and seek out the aforesaid parts."
JACOBA FELICIE, 1322

LABOR PAINS

Alleviating the pain of childbirth was considered sinful by many clergymen. One Scottish clergyman said it was "vitiating the primal curse against woman." In America, chloroform was labeled "a decoy of Satan." Such criticism was finally quashed when Queen Victoria gave her doctor, John Snow, permission to administer chloroform during the birth of her eighth child, Prince Leopold, in 1853. Subsequently this method became known as *anesthésie à la reine.*

"For the speedy delivery of women in child bed. Take the liver of an Eel killed in the full of the Moon (by reason the Moon hath such a very great influence over women). Dry it in the light of the Moon as much as possible you can without moulding: then in the Sun. Then bruise it to a fine powder and give it to the party in white wine: it will ease her pain."
From MARY WILLIAM'S BOOK, 1656

ADVICE FOR MIDWIVES

Trotula, a female physician at the thirteenth-century University of Salerno, in Italy, gave straightforward advice to midwives concerning the repositioning of the unborn infant during labor:

"If the child does not come forth in the order in which it should, that is if the legs or arms should come out first, let the midwife with her small and gentle hand moistened with a decoction of flaxseed and chick peas, put the child back in its place in the proper position."

A HIGH CALLING

"Nursing is said, most truly said, to be a high calling, an honourable calling. But what does the honour lie in? In working hard during your training to learn and to do all things perfectly. The honour does not lie in putting on Nursing like your uniform, your dress… Honour lies in loving perfection, consistency, and in working hard for it; in being ready to work patiently: ready to say not 'How clever I am!' but 'I am not yet worthy; and I will live to deserve and work to deserve to be called a Trained Nurse.'"

FLORENCE NIGHTINGALE (1820-1910)

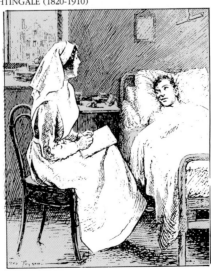

A MEDICAL VOCATION

"Although women make the best nurses, they do not inspire confidence as doctors since their judgement varies from month to month."
DR. HORATIO STORER, NINETEENTH CENTURY

Although there were many women physicians in the ancient world, as time wore on the medical profession became more and more structured. Increasing emphasis was laid on official examination results and recognized qualifications, and women found it harder and harder to gain acceptance in the profession. Dr. Elizabeth Blackwell – who attended the Geneva Medical College in New York, and is recorded as the first-ever modern woman to have graduated as a doctor, in 1849 – described the difficulties facing female graduates in the mid nineteenth century:

"A blank wall of social and professional antagonism faces the woman physician that forms a situation of painful loneliness, leaving her without support, respect or professional counsel."

Despite such opposition, however, women were undeterred and many went on to great success in medical careers through their own determination, courage, and sheer hard work.

THE GLITTERING PRIZES

Marie Curie (1867-1934) began her illustrious scientific career as a governess. But this did not prevent her from studying:

"At nine in the evening I take my books and go to work… I have even acquired the habit of getting up at six so that I work more – but I can't always do it."

Later, she had to combine her work with motherhood and the care of her two daughters. She wrote:

"I have a great deal of work, what with the housekeeping, the children, the teaching and the laboratory."

Her extraordinary dedication brought extraordinary rewards. She was to win two Nobel Prizes; the first, acknowledging her work on radioactivity, was shared with her husband, Pierre, and Henri Becquerel in 1903; her second, for chemistry, came in 1911. She was the first person to be honored twice in this way.

CHAPTER TWO
WOMEN IN LOVE
=)•••••••••(=

Man's love is of man's life a thing apart,
'Tis woman's whole existence.
From DON JUAN by LORD BYRON (1788-1824)

THE JOYS AND SORROWS OF LOVE REMAIN LITTLE CHANGED
ACROSS THE CENTURIES. WOMEN AND MEN HAVE LOVED AND
LOST, AND LOVED AGAIN, FOR THOUSANDS OF YEARS; AND YET
MOST OF US ARE STILL UNENLIGHTENED AS TO THE TRUE
NATURE OF THIS COMPELLING EMOTION. THAT LOVE IS BLIND
AND CAPRICIOUS IS PERHAPS SOMETHING ON WHICH BOTH
SEXES AGREE; THAT LOVE IS ESSENTIALLY A FEMININE MYSTERY
WITH THE POWER TO TRANSFORM AN INDIVIDUAL FOR
GOOD OR ILL IS PERHAPS ANOTHER.

Nothing is sweeter than love, all other blessings
Come second to it. I have spat even honey
From my mouth – I, Nossis,
Say this is so. But one whom Kypris
Has not loved, will never know
What roses her flowers are.

NOSSIS OF LOCRI (WOMAN POET, THIRD CENTURY B.C.)

KYPRIS Another name for Aphrodite, Greek goddess of love.

THE GAME OF LOVE

Like the games and battles to which it is compared,
love requires strategy – an essentially female art.

"Now it needs no very brilliant discernment to perceive
that when once the woman has a man in love with her,
she holds in her hands a tremendous power for her
own advantage. In the first place, whether rich or poor,
young or old, handsome or plain, a devoted admirer
is always useful to a woman. She can, by means of
him, bring others to her feet: for one of Man's most
noticeable weaknesses is the impulse to follow a leader;
and we women have an unspoken proverb: 'Lovers
never come singly.'… It is, therefore, a most important
thing for a woman to have a hanger-on… for such are
harmless and interfere very little in the game."

From "THE TRUTH ABOUT MAN BY A SPINSTER," LADY'S REALM MAGAZINE, 1904

WANTED: THE IDEAL MAN

Woman's image of the "dream man" seems timeless: in
this poem, an anonymous woman listed the attributes
expected of a "Prince Charming" in medieval France:

Maiden, if he really wants my love,
He'll have to show high spirits and behave,
Be frank and humble, not pick fights with any man,
Be courteous with everyone;
For I don't want a man who's proud or bitter,
Who'll debase my worth or ruin me,
But one who's frank and noble, loving and discreet…

FREE LOVE

In pre-Roman Italy, Etruscan women led lives of great sexual license and freedom. They were said to be both remarkably beautiful and, according to one classical source, "terribly bibulous." They often chose their lovers on a whim, and proceeded to consummate their romantic feelings with fearless frankness and breathtaking immediacy. Consequently, all their offspring were brought up as equals, as no one could be sure of their parentage.

"It is no disgrace for Etruscans to be seen doing anything in the open, or even having anything done to them, for this, too, is a custom of the country."
From THE SAGES AT DINNER by ATHENAEUS, FIFTH CENTURY B.C.

APHRODITE'S MONTH

The month of April is said to be named for the Greek goddess of love, Aphrodite. Remnants of her worship can still be glimpsed in contemporary May Day celebrations, since May Day is an ancient fertility festival celebrating the wedding of the goddess to her consort. Traditionally the festivities began on May Eve (the night of April 30th) with wild parties in the woods – much to the disgust of the Puritan Philip Stubbes, who was clearly appalled by such pagan debauchery:

"I have heard it credibly reported by men of great gravity, credit and reputation; that of forty, threescore or a hundred maids going to the wood over night, there have scarcely the third part of them returned home again undefiled."
From THE ANATOMY OF ABUSES by PHILIP STUBBES, 1586

STAYING BEAUTIFUL

"Being a sex symbol is a heavy load to carry, especially when one is tired, hurt, and bewildered."
MARILYN MONROE (1926-62)

For thousands of years, women have endeavored both to stay attractive and to improve on nature. A beautiful woman enjoys a certain transient power – in many societies the only power she might ever wield.

Women who became the mistresses of influential men worked as hard as any modern film star at their appearance, since their position depended upon it. Others, whether commoners or royalty, also devoted much energy to the pursuit of physical perfection. Some of their practices were wildly extravagant; others could form the basis of natural remedies today.

"Any girl can be glamorous. All you have to do is stand still and look stupid."
HEDY LAMARR (b. 1913)

STRAWBERRIES FOR THE SKIN

Lady Emma Hamilton, the incorrigible mistress of Admiral Nelson, is said to have had ravishing skin and a great fondness for brandy – on which she based her recipe for an astringent lotion for oily skin. To make it, she would first steep fresh strawberries in half a pint of brandy for a week. The brandy would then be strained, and more strawberries and half an ounce of camphor added. After a further week, the mixture would be strained again and was then ready for use.

CAMPHOR An aromatic oil, derived from the camphor tree.

THE ROYAL BATH

Both Catherine the Great of Russia (1729-96) and Madame de Pompadour (1721-64) believed in the beneficial qualities of herbs. The Russian queen took lengthy herbal baths each day, and employed a team of men to travel throughout Europe and the Far East, searching for suitable herbs and flowers.

Madame de Pompadour, who became the mistress of Louis XV of France when she was twenty-four, also engaged dozens of men for the same purpose. She loved to be surrounded by scented flowers, especially hyacinths. Her baths were so frequent that her royal lover feared for her health, and begged her to desist. However, she ignored his pleas – and also those of his physicians, who believed bathing was dangerous.

The French queen Marie Antoinette used to add an infusion of thyme, marjoram, bay leaves, and sea salt to her bath, and Mary, Queen of Scots, preferred to bathe in wine.

MILK BATHS

The most legendary exponent of the milk bath must be Cleopatra, the ultimate seductress, who is said to have bathed in asses' milk.

Novelist George Sand (1804-76) – who defied convention by leaving her husband to live with a series of lovers, including the composer Chopin, and the poet Alfred de Musset – favored milk baths to preserve and moisturize her skin. Her bath recipe is sufficient for a very large bath indeed:

"Dissolve 3 ounces of bicarbonate of soda and 8 ounces of kitchen salt in a quart of water. Dissolve 3 pounds of honey in 3 quarts of milk. Pour the soda and salt solution into the bath, mix, and stir in the milk and honey."

SUFFERING TO BE BEAUTIFUL

Extreme measures have always been favored by some misguided women who have subjected themselves to forms of voluntary torture in a pitiful quest for an exquisite appearance.

Tight-laced corsets prevailed for centuries, causing breathing difficulties, bruising, and general lassitude. One Victorian advertisement, for the "Whalonia" belted corset, reads: "These long-waisted Corsets have a small demi-belt inserted, made of Silk Elastic, which relieves all pressure on the vital and delicate organs and gives, without tight lacing, an elegant and graceful figure not obtainable in ordinary makes."

"Beauty has been my curse."
HEDY LAMARR (b. 1913)

PALE HANDS

Lovely hands were considered the epitome of femininity in nineteenth-century Spain. Lola Montez, an infamous dancer, adventuress, and sometime mistress of King Ludwig of Bavaria, noted an extreme practice amongst her female contemporaries. Some of these women actually slept with their hands hoisted above their heads by pulleys, in the hope of "rendering them pale and delicate." The less fanatical resorted to a pomade made from soap, salad oil, mutton tallow, and spirits of wine which they plastered over their hands at night, donning a pair of gloves to keep the bedclothes clean.

GENTLEMEN PREFER BLONDES

The Contessa Nani, who lived in sixteenth-century Venice, wrote a book of cosmetic recipes, including an alarming concoction intended to dye the hair blonde. This consisted of a mixture of sulphur, alum, honey, and water, applied to the hair, which was then dried in the sun. More timid Venetian souls favored a mixture of lemon juice and dung. Wearing a *solana*, a special crownless hat with a huge brim over which to spread the hair, they would sit on their rooftops until their hair was bleached to the red-gold shade immortalized by the painter Titian.

THE SINGLE LIFE

Throughout history, some women have elected to remain single – through choice, religious belief, or the simple lack of the right man at the right time. Some felt alone and incomplete, others exulted in their "maiden" status.

> *"Men are my hobby.*
> *If I ever got married, I'd have to give it up."*
> MAE WEST (1892-1980)

IN PRAISE OF OLDER WOMEN

Diane de Poitiers was the beloved mistress of the young King Henry II of France. Some years younger than she, he was one of history's first "toyboys." Diane bathed in rainwater and walked in the rain to improve her skin. When not attending royal banquets, she believed in a light vegetarian diet which, she said, helped her keep both complexion and figure.

> *"The years that a woman subtracts from her age are*
> *not lost. They are added to the ages of other women."*
> DIANE DE POITIERS (1499-1566)

A SPINSTER'S REBELLION

"Being an old maid is like death by drowning, a really delightful sensation after you cease to struggle."
EDNA FERBER (1887-1968)

In Victorian times, a respectable woman had few options in matters of love – either she married, or remained single and celibate. If she had not found a husband by the age of thirty, she was "on the shelf," where she was likely to remain for the rest of her days. The idea of having lovers and children outside of wedlock was unthinkable, something done only by those euphemistically called "fallen women." Single women who managed to remain virtuous were termed "old maids" or spinsters, and expected to lead lives of dutiful servitude. But sometimes rebellion stirred:

"Why it should be customary to speak of women of thirty or upwards in tones of pity, sometimes a little mixed with contempt, because they do not happen to be married, certainly strikes me as odd. I freely allow that the married state is the happier for both men and women, if it really is a thorough union of hearts, as well as fortunes. In so many cases, however, it is nothing of the kind, and then I think the wife has cause to envy, and not to commiserate her maiden sister. The more I think about it, the more foolish it seems to me to pity a woman simply because she is unwed. Who pities the bachelor for the same reason? The very idea is absurd."
From HOME NOTES MAGAZINE by "ISOBEL," 1894

FALLEN WOMEN

While prostitutes led miserable, oppressed lives, many courtesans were examples of sexual and emotional emancipation. Courtesans were, throughout history, witty, educated companions as well as mistresses. Their sexual freedom was linked with economic freedom, for their lovers invariably gave them houses, land, jewelry, and other valuable gifts – while wives had nothing to call their own, as they were financially dependent on their husbands. Of course, courtesans had to put up with moral censure, and the prospect of growing old disgracefully.

DOUBLE TROUBLE

Since virginity was such a highly-prized commodity in the marriage market, a woman was considered "soiled" once she had lost this precious possession – despite the fact that she was not solely responsible for its loss.

Many young women, seduced as adolescents, were indeed "ruined," for they went on to lead lives of utter degradation and misery. Others, like the admirable Cora Pearl (1835-86), turned their bewilderment and rage to more positive account.

Cora became a courtesan following her seduction as a very young girl. Despite her early experience – of which she wrote angrily in her memoirs – her un-bowed spirit and enormous vitality stood her in good stead, and she went on to make an outrageous career in Paris as an extravagant *grande horizontale*. She prized her hard-earned autonomy, stating: "I have never deceived anybody, because I have never belonged to anybody."

"It takes two to get one into trouble."
MAE WEST (1892-1980)

UNDERSTANDING MEN

"A woman we love rarely satisfies all our needs, and we deceive her with a woman whom we do not love."
MARCEL PROUST (1871-1922)

Every generation of women believes that relationships must have been different for their grandmothers and great-grandmothers. Brought up on exquisite tales of true love, women find it difficult to reconcile puzzling masculine behavior with apparent reality. Comfort may, however, be gained from the knowledge that such confusion is seemingly eternal. As long ago as the tenth century, the Japanese courtesan Sei Shonagon described men's emotions as "strange," and thought their behavior in matters of love was "bizarre."

Nine hundred years later, little seems to have changed. An anonymous female journalist, writing in the early twentieth century, appears to have had much in common with her Japanese counterpart, for she made the following observation:

"It is not the passion itself that I have to bring up against Man the mature; it is the remarkable brevity of that passion... We never expect the sudden volte-face, the unwonted coolness and dignity, the rapid leap from the torrid to the frigid zone, that is one of Man's most extraordinary phenomena."
From "THE TRUTH ABOUT MAN," LADY'S REALM MAGAZINE, 1904

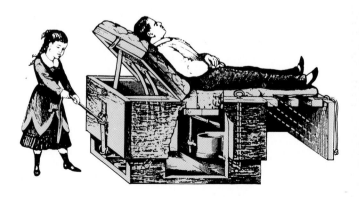

CHAPTER THREE

MARRIAGE & MOTHERHOOD

*"One of the oldest human needs is having someone to
wonder where you are when you
don't come home at night."*

MARGARET MEAD (1901-78)

*THOSE TWIN RITES OF PASSAGE, MARRIAGE AND MOTHERHOOD,
REMAIN OF THE UTMOST SIGNIFICANCE.
MOTHERHOOD ITSELF, BY ITS VERY NATURE, HAS ALTERED LITTLE,
BUT MARRIAGE IS INEVITABLY NOT QUITE THE INSTITUTION
IT ONCE WAS.*

MODES OF MARRIAGE

"Marriage is the woman's proper sphere, her divinely ordered place, her natural end. It is what she is born for, what she is trained for, what she is exhibited for. It is, moreover, her means of honorable livelihood and advancement. But she must not ever look as if she wanted it!"

CHARLOTTE PERKINS GILMAN (1860-1935)

MARRIAGE IN SPARTA

In ancient Sparta a remarkably liberal code prevailed, and Spartan wives enjoyed an enviable freedom. A married woman of sufficient means frequently ran two households, which she owned, keeping a different husband in each. Wives could also take lovers, subject to their husband's approval – and vice versa. Should the wife have a child by her lover, the original husband willingly accepted the infant as his own.

MARRIAGE IN ANCIENT ROME

Roman law recognized three forms of marriage:

- *Conferatio,* which was a simple religious ceremony.
- *Coemptio,* whereby a girl was "sold" to her husband by her father.
- *Usus,* whereby a couple who had lived together for a year were automatically regarded as married.

MARRIAGE IN ANCIENT BRITAIN

When the Roman general Julius Caesar invaded Britain in 55 B.C., he was fascinated by the marriage arrangements of the inhabitants. In his book describing the campaign, he reported that:

"Wives are shared between groups of ten or twelve men, especially between brothers and between fathers and sons; but the offspring of these unions are counted as the children of the man with whom a particular woman cohabited first."

MARRIAGE IN ANCIENT JAPAN

The archaic Japanese word for marriage meant "to slip into the house by night," and referred to the fact that until about 1400 A.D. Japanese husbands did not live with their wives and merely visited them.

TRIAL MARRIAGE

There are many old customs that suggest trial marriages were a common event. These echo ancient practices in which the goddess of love chose a "husband" each year, rapidly disposing of his predecessor.

"At the Lammas Fair, it was the custom for unmarried persons of both sexes to choose a companion, according to their liking, with whom they were to live till that time next year. This was called Hand-fasting, or hand-in-fist. If they were pleased with each other, then they continued together for life; if not, they separated and were free to make another choice."
OLD STATISTICAL ACCOUNT, PARISH OF ESKDALEMUIR, 1749

Other evocative names for this practice include:

- Tarrying
- Night-visiting
- Courting-on-the-bed.

CHILD BRIDES

Many brides were as young as twelve, or even younger, when they were betrothed. In eighth-century France, a law was passed banning marriage before that age, because "it appears to us that girls are not mature before they have completed twelve years."

Child brides in ancient Greece went to the temple and made a special dedication before their wedding day. This one marks a poignant farewell to childhood:

"Timareta before her wedding has dedicated to you, Artemis of the Lake, her tambourine, her pretty ball and the caul that upheld her hair, her dolls too, and their dresses: a virgin's gift, as is right to a Virgin. Artemis, hold your hand above the girl and purely preserve her in her purity."

EARNING A DOWRY

The exchange of goods and property is a traditional part of the marriage bargain, and in many cultures the bride is expected to come complete with her own dowry. The problem of how to pay for the dowry has been nicely solved by the women of the Ouled Nail, a tribe living in the Algerian Sahara: they dance for their dowries. After training from infancy, they begin their "careers" when about twelve years old. They travel from oasis to oasis, turning most of their earnings into jewelry, so that by the time they retire they are loaded with bracelets and necklaces of gold and silver.

WHAT TO EXPECT IN A HUSBAND

In ancient Britain, a wife's expectations of her husband may have been somewhat different from those of today, for the English word "husband" means "one bonded to the house" – which, in those days, invariably belonged to the wife. The word "husbandry" still retains its original meaning, referring to work on the land, a responsibility which a husband took up upon marriage.

CHOOSING THE RIGHT MAN

In choosing whom she wishes to marry, a would-be bride is well advised to heed the words of those who have learned from experience:

"An archaeologist is the best husband any woman can have: the older she gets, the more interested he is in her."
AGATHA CHRISTIE (1890-1976)

"I think every woman's entitled to a middle husband she can forget."
ADELA ROGERS ST. JOHNS (1894-1988)

"Husbands are like fires. They go out when unattended."
ZSA ZSA GABOR (b.1919)

WHEN TO MARRY

Marry in September's shine,
Your living will be rich and fine;
If in October you do marry,
Love will come but riches tarry;
If you wed in bleak November,
Only joy will come, remember;
When December's showers fall fast,
Marry and true love will last.
TRADITIONAL RHYME

Many of the superstitions about the timing of the wedding were originally pagan strictures, from ancient religions. Long ago a woman's wisdom in such matters was part of her birthright. Even today much folklore attaches to the wedding, and also to the bride herself.

Monday for wealth,
Tuesday for health,
Wednesday the best day of all;
Thursday for crosses,
Friday for losses,
Saturday no luck at all.
TRADITIONAL RHYME

WHEN NOT TO MARRY

In Europe, marriages were banned between Advent, at the beginning of December, and on St. Hilary's Day, which falls on January 13th. Lent, the forty-day period of abstinence prior to Easter, was another time when weddings were not encouraged.

For centuries, May was also considered an unlucky month for marriages, a month when witches flew in the skies and fairies were abroad. It was a time of great celebration, welcoming spring in all its glory and fertility. The taboo may have its origins in pagan traditions, for May was the month when the goddess of love chose her "husband" for the year to come. All over Europe this festival was commemorated with dances around the Maypole, and adult revels in the woods and fields on May Eve.

"Maids are May when they are maids, but the sky changes when they are wives."
WILLIAM SHAKESPEARE (1564-1616)

ON THE SPUR OF THE MOMENT

"I did a most crazy thing. Some time ago I married Charley Burke. He got me in a weak moment & we were married. He is a good man, honest & on the square, but I don't love him, dear. I am still in love with your Father Bill Hickok. But Charley is near my own age, dark haired, blue eyed. Marriage isn't all a romance, either. We were married down by the river under a clump of cottonwood trees. Janey, the sunshine crept softly down between the tree branches seeming to spread a glory of radiant light about the group of friends gathering there. The sunshine was like a benediction. Of course I cried. I'm always bawling."
CALAMITY JANE TO HER DAUGHTER JANEY, 1891

ADVICE FOR BRIDES

According to folklore, a bride must observe the following advice if she is to be happily married.

SHE SHOULD NOT
- Break anything on her wedding, as that foretells strife.
- Try on either her wedding dress or her veil on her wedding morning.
- Try on her wedding ring before the ceremony.
- Look at herself in the mirror once she has finished dressing for her wedding.
- Lose the heel of her shoe, or she will be unable to get on with her husband's relatives.
- Read the marriage service through.
- See the bridegroom before she meets him in church.
- Keep back her tears (so she will have wept them all away).
- Wear pearls, as they mean tears.
- Touch rags.
- See a pin on the ground as she leaves the church.
- Stumble on the threshold of the church.
- Forget to feed the cat, otherwise it may spite her by bringing down rain.
- Have an encounter with a hare, a dog, a cat, a lizard, a pig, or a funeral.

SHE SHOULD
- Try to engineer an encounter with a spider, a frog, a lamb, a dove, or a songbird.
- Tell her elder or unmarried sisters to wear green stockings, or they will never be married themselves.

WHAT TO WEAR

Married in white, you have chosen all right.
Married in green, ashamed to be seen.
Married in grey, you will go far away.
Married in red, you will wish yourself dead.
Married in blue, he will ever be true.
Married in yellow, ashamed of the fellow.
Married in black, comforts you'll lack.
Married in pink, your spirits will sink.
Married in brown, you'll live out of town.
Married in pearl, you'll live in a whirl.

TRADITIONAL RHYME

At different times and in different cultures, brides have opted for a variety of wedding attire.

Sicilian brides traditionally wore a multi-colored dress for the wedding, and a garland of orange blossoms to symbolize fertility.

In Russia, a young girl wore one plait. For her wedding day, her hair was braided into two plaits to signify her forthcoming status as a wife.

Vervain, or verbena, was once sacred to Venus. German brides wore a crown made of this herb, echoing classical tradition.

If a woman married in her shift – usually a kind of linen vest – she was said to free her future husband from liability for debts accrued before the wedding.

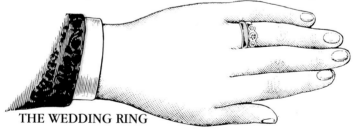

THE WEDDING RING

"The form of the wedding ring being circular, that is round and without end, imparteth thus much, that their mutual love and affection should roundly flow from one to the other as in a circle, and that continually and forever."

From THE TREATISE OF SPOUSALS by HENRY SWINBURNE, 1686

BRIDAL CEREMONY

An Arab bride goes to her wedding protected, purified, and enhanced by henna. A thick green powder is made from henna leaves, which yields a deep-red dye. Mixed with water, this paste is applied to her hair, and intricate designs are painted on her hands and feet by her female friends and relations. Once these ritual decorations have been completed, all the women dance together in an exuberant ancient ceremony that excludes men.

BONNY AND BUXOM

The familiar words of the Anglican marriage ceremony are based on an Anglo-Saxon tradition in which the bride's land was ceremonially transferred to the stewardship of her husband. At the ceremony, the bridegroom vowed:

"With this ring I thee wed, and this gold and silver I give thee, and with my body I thee worship, and with all my worldly chattels I thee honour."

To which the bride replied:

"I take thee to my wedded husband, to have and to hold, for fairer for fouler, for better for worse, for richer for poorer, in sickness and in health, to be bonny and buxom in bed and at board, till death us do part."

TO CHERISH AND OBEY

In ancient Egypt, a wife was held in high esteem, and wielded considerable material and emotional power, as revealed by this formal vow made by one husband:

"I bow before thy rights as a wife. From this day on, I shall never oppose thy claims with a single word. I recognize thee before all others as my wife, though I do not have the right to say thou must be my wife. Only I am thy husband and mate. Thou alone hast the right of departure. From this day on that I have become thy husband, I cannot oppose thy wish, wherever thou desirest to go ... I have no power to interfere in any of thy transactions. I hereby cede to thee any rights deeded to me in any document that has been made out in my favour. Thou keepest me obligated to recognize all these cessions."

Similarly, husbands were advised on their behavior by the priests, who counseled them as follows:

"Keep thy house, love thy wife, and do not dispute with her. She will withdraw herself before violence. Feed her, adorn her, massage her. Caress her and make her heart to rejoice as long as thou livest ... Attend to that which is her desire and to that which occupies her mind. For in such manner thou persuadest her to remain with thee. If thou opposest her, it will be thy ruin."

THE SCRIBE ANI, ANCIENT EGYPT

THE MARRIAGE OAK

For centuries it was customary for newly-married couples to dance around an oak tree known as the "marriage oak." This ceremony was said to bring them luck. Its origins lie in the sacred groves of the great mother goddesses such as Demeter or Diana, where an imposing tree symbolized the goddess's consort.

WEDDING FEASTS

The timeless significance of food at a wedding is clearly linked to fertility rites, and the symbolic wish that the happy couple should never go hungry.

CORN AND CONFETTI
Pagan brides wore symbolic ears of corn on their wedding day to ensure fertility and as a tribute to the corn goddess. Eventually, the presence of corn at a wedding was replaced by little cakes, which were broken up and scattered over the couple as they left the church. Today, paper confetti remains a reminder of this ancient rite.

BRIDAL SHOWER
The first thing a Greek bride did upon entering her new home was to crush a pomegranate, sacred to the goddess Persephone, and mark a butter cross on the doorpost. As she and her husband climbed the stairs to their bedroom, they were showered with chick-peas, barley, rice, sweets, and coins to encourage abundance and fertility in their marriage.

OATMEAL
In Ireland the couple were presented with a dish of oatmeal and salt, to symbolize the basic necessities of life and protect them from the Evil Eye.

HUGGING BONE
In Scotland the bride and groom shared a chicken at their wedding breakfast. Once the bird had been eaten, the bride was given a small side bone to bring her happiness. This bone went by the charming name of "hug me close."

BITTERSWEET OFFERING
In the Netherlands the bridal couple were offered salty cream sprinkled with sugar. This represented the bitter and sweet aspects of marriage.

WEDDING CAKE

The traditional wedding cake, which combines sweet fruits, icing, and bitter almonds, symbolizes the fruitfulness, richness, and bittersweet nature of marriage.

Single women were encouraged to take a slice home, and sleep with it beneath their pillows. This little ritual was supposed to ensure that a woman would dream of her future husband. In Yorkshire, in northern England, wedding cake was called "dreaming bread" for this reason.

TILL DEATH US DO PART

Before the advent of Islam, if her marriage looked as if it was not going to last "till death us do part," an Arab wife had an option open to her that was much easier and cheaper than the modern divorce. All she had to do to divorce her husband was to turn her tent so that it faced west for three consecutive nights.

A similar custom prevailed in the Mediterranean: the husband was simply barred from entering the house for three nights in a row.

A CURIOUS BARGAIN

As late as the nineteenth century, a curious "divorce" custom prevailed in some parts of England, as witness the following report:

"They came into the market between ten and eleven o'clock in the morning, the woman being led by a halter which was fastened round her neck and the middle of her body. In a few minutes after their arrival she was sold to a man of the name of Thomas Snape, a nailer of Burntwood. The purchase money was two shillings and sixpence, and all the parties seemed satisfied with the bargain. The husband was glad to get rid of his frail rib, who, it seems, had been living with Snape three years."

From THE WOLVERHAMPTON CHRONICLE, 1837

BECOMING A MOTHER

*"Making the decision to have a child is momentous.
It is to decide forever to have your heart go walking
around outside your body."*
ELIZABETH STONE

A new mother was considered "unclean" until she had been purified and blessed by the Church. In Ireland and Scotland, she was not allowed to leave her house until this ritual had been performed, as she was believed to be unlucky. To circumvent this tedious restriction, Irish women fastened a straw from their roof (if it was thatched) or a splinter of slate to their hats – then, with true Celtic logic, they could claim that they had never left the shelter of their own roof.

"Only a mother knows a mother's fondness."
LADY MARY WORTLEY MONTAGU (1689-1762)

CHANGELINGS

Stories abound of mothers going home with the wrong baby. Such tales are timeless, and long ago women took precautions against being saddled with a fairy child. In Scotland, a mother would settle the baby close to the hearth fire. If it was indeed a changeling child, it was expected to fly away up the chimney.

Wedding Cake.

ROYAL BIRTHS

A royal heir was of infinite importance, and serious ceremonies attended the occasion of royal motherhood. In sixteenth-century France, Queen Marie de Médicis gave birth on a red velvet birthing stool. In attendance were the King and the Princes of the Blood, supplemented by praying nuns and a selection of religious relics, including the Virgin Mary's belt.

Ill-fated Anne Boleyn, second wife of Henry VIII of England, was escorted in the first stages of her labor to special rooms by the Lord Chamberlain and her ladies-in-waiting. A mass was celebrated there, and the queen took communion. Unfortunately, she produced a daughter, Mary – and her failure to present Henry with the required son led to her execution.

Another unlucky queen, Marie Antoinette, was overwhelmed by the huge number of courtiers present at the birth of her first child in 1770. Some of them even climbed on the furniture in order to gain a better view of the infant's entry to the world. Following a successful birth, she fainted, and was revived by being bled from the foot – although the fact that the king opened some windows and ejected the crowd may also have contributed to her recovery.

Queen Mab

WHAT'S IN A NAME?

Names have always held a certain magical, mystical significance – and the naming of a new-born baby is still an extremely special moment.

SOUL NAME

Gypsies have kept an ancient tradition alive to this day – the mother whispers a secret name to her infant when it first suckles at her breast. This ritual is repeated at puberty, and remains a secret between mother and child, for this hidden name is said to protect the child's soul throughout life. The ancient Egyptians followed the same custom.

RICE NAME

In China, children received their secret soul name when they were weaned and ate their first dish of rice. It was called a "rice name."

MILK NAME

In France, mothers gave their child a *nom de lait*, or milk name, that was different from its other names.

HONOR THY MOTHER

*"Ask your child what he wants for dinner
only if he's buying."*
FRAN LEBOWITZ (b. 1951)

*"Being a mother is a noble status, right?
Right. So why does it change when you put 'unwed'
or 'welfare' in front of it?"*
FLORENCE R. KENNEDY (b. 1916)

When the Ten Commandments exhorted everyone to "honor thy father and thy mother," they were only echoing something fundamental in human nature. But before people realized there was a link between conception and pregnancy the emphasis was, naturally, on honoring thy mother:

"Thou shalt never forget thy mother and what she has done for thee. For she carried thee long beneath her heart as a heavy burden, and after thy months were accomplished she bore thee. Three long years she carried thee upon her shoulder and gave thee her breast to thy mouth, and as thy size increased her heart never once allowed her to say, 'Why should I do this?' "
EGYPTIAN SCRIPTURE, 1500 B.C.

Chapter Four

A Woman's Place

*"Some respite to husbands the weather may send,
But housewives' affairs have never an end."*

From FIVE HUNDRED POINTS OF GOOD HUSBANDRY
by THOMAS TUSSER (c.1524-80)

*FOR THOUSANDS OF YEARS, HEARTH AND HOME HAVE BEEN
WOMEN'S PROVINCE. NOW FREQUENTLY SEEN AS A PLACE
OF CONFINEMENT, THE HOME WAS FORMERLY REGARDED AS A
REFUGE, AND A SOURCE OF COMFORT AND SPIRITUAL
NOURISHMENT. PRIOR TO THE GREAT DIVISION BETWEEN
"WORK" AND "HOME," EVERYONE'S DAILY LIFE REVOLVED
AROUND HIS OR HER DWELLING PLACE AND
ITS SURROUNDING LAND.*

BLESS THIS HOUSE

Our pattern of life has radically altered since the Industrial Revolution. Before that time, most people lived and worked in the same place for generations – both on the land and in the towns. Women made homes, tended the sacred hearth fires, and very often owned both land and property. In societies as diverse as ancient Egypt, Celtic Britain, Babylonia and ancient Greece, a woman's home was truly her pride and joy.

I went sunways round my dwelling
In the name of Mother Mary
Who promised to preserve me
Who did protect me
Who will preserve me
In peace, in flocks, in righteousness of heart.

TRADITIONAL GAELIC PRAYER
TO BLESS THE HOME AT THE FEAST OF THE ASSUMPTION

KEEP THE HOME FIRES BURNING

For centuries, the hearth, with its warming fire, has been associated with the comfort and security of home and, by extension, with the nurturing female figure – wife and mother – around whom the home revolved. The ancient Greeks considered the hearth worthy of its own deity, and assigned to it Hestia, goddess of the hearth (her Roman equivalent was Vesta). Hestia tended the sacred fire on Mount Olympus, home of the gods, and every town and city kept a community hearth fire perpetually burning in her honor. Hestia's strength and importance were such that she was one of the few Olympians said to be immune to the countless tricks played by Aphrodite, goddess of love.

"Here's to the maiden of bashful fifteen;
Here's to the widow of fifty;
Here's to the flaunting extravagant quean,
And here's to the housewife that's thrifty.
Let the toast pass,
Drink to the lass,
I'll warrant she'll prove an excuse for the glass."

From THE SCHOOL FOR SCANDAL by R.B. SHERIDAN (1751-1816)

THE HEART OF THE HOME

"Few housewives realize what powers they possess and
how much depends on them; how they have within
their grasp to make or mar the lives of everyone within
the household. They are the pivot – the centre around
which this small organisation works and when it is out
of gear everything is affected."

WOMAN'S OWN MAGAZINE, 1932

The silent and often unrecognized contribution made
by women to the well-being and happiness of their
families was acknowledged as far back as ancient
Egypt, in these touching words by the scribe Ani:

"Be not rude to a woman in her house if you know her
thoroughly. Do not say, 'Where is that? Bring it to me!',
when she has put it in its right place and your eye has
not seen it. When you are silent, you know her qualities
and it is a joy for your hand to be with her."

THE GOOD HOUSEWIFE

A housewife has always been a woman who ran the
home. Before the days of commercial food production,
however, her job involved more than just cooking and
cleaning. She had to grow her own vegetables and
herbs for the kitchen, and care for livestock, too –
perhaps a cow, a pig, and a flock of hens.

DUTIES OF A HOUSEWIFE

Running a home requires diverse skills. In fourteenth-century Paris, the young wife of one French husband, known only as the "Ménagier," was instructed by him in her duties. He thoughtfully wrote her a book containing a mass of information – from simple stain removal to organizing a banquet for forty guests. Arcane tasks included filling hourglasses with marble dust and making rosewater for the wash-basins.

"In my opinion a lady of condition should learn just as much of cooking and of washing as to know when she is imposed upon by those she employs."
THE FEMALE SPECTATOR by ELIZA HAYWOOD (1690-1756)

"Go to your apartments, lady, and take your ease; drink pleasant draughts to fatten your body. Think out for your household what they shall eat and drink, and meddle not with other things."
RAOUL (THIRTEENTH CENTURY)

"No woman should allow her brother to put on linen in a state of dilapidation, to wear gloves or stockings in want of mending, or to return home without finding a neat parlour, a place to sit down without asking for it, and a cheerful invitation to partake of necessary refreshment."
From WOMEN OF ENGLAND by SARAH STICKNEY ELLIS, 1839

"Every woman should learn to be a good sanitary officer for the home. She should know what a healthy house is, and how to keep it so. Every room must be clean and full of fresh air. Fresh bright colourings in the decorations have a good effect on the mind and health of the occupants of the house."
From HINTS PRINTED ON GIRL GUIDE BADGES by MRS. JANSON POTTS, 1940

THE COOK.   THE NURSE.   THE HOUSEMAID.

HOUSEWORK

There was an old woman tossed up in a blanket,
Seventeen times as high as the moon;
Where she was going I could not but ask it,
For in her hand she carried a broom.

"Old woman, old woman, old woman," quoth I;
"O whither, O whither, O whither so high?"
"To sweep the cob-webs from the sky,
And I'll be with you by-and-by!"

TRADITIONAL NURSERY RHYME

Depending on their financial status, women have found various solutions for dealing with the many tasks involved in running a home. The wealthier ones have always been able to pay for servants to help lighten the load:

"As soon as she is able to afford it she hires a washer-
woman occasionally, then a charwoman, then a cook
and housemaid, a nurse or two, a governess, a lady's
maid, a housekeeper – and no blame attaches to
any step of her progress unless the payment is beyond
her means."

ANONYMOUS, 1870

SUPERWOMEN

Less fortunate women have had to manage myriad tasks alone – although their responsibilities did not quite extend to keeping the sky clean. Undaunted, they have often emerged as "superwomen," displaying an impressive array of skills and a level of organizational ability equal to that of the most high-powered of businessmen. The range of responsibilities such women have had to handle seems to have altered little over the centuries, as revealed in the words of one thoroughly disgruntled housewife in ancient Greece:

"It is difficult for a woman to get out, what with dancing attendance on her husband, or getting the servant girl up, or putting the child to bed, or bathing the brat, or feeding it…"

From LYSISTRATA by ARISTOPHANES, 411 B.C.

WOMEN'S WORK

Another alternative for the hard-pressed housewife was to enlist her husband's help, but this had its drawbacks. Even if the husband agreed, there could be strong disapproval in other quarters. In the eyes of many, housework was decidedly women's work, and not something that any self-respecting man should be caught doing. Those men who dared to be different did so at their own peril. At the turn of the century in the north of England, men who helped women with the housework were scornfully nicknamed "diddy men" or "mop rags."

> *Man for the field and woman for the hearth;*
> *Man for the sword and for the needle she…*
> *All else confusion…*
>
> From PRINCESS IDA by ALFRED, LORD TENNYSON, 1847

ALL IN A DAY'S WORK

Like all other practical tasks, routine simplifies house-work. Few modern women, however, have either the time or inclination to follow the elaborate routines of the past. Writing earlier this century, a Miss A.M. Kaye advised the housewife that certain tasks should be attended to every day. These consisted of:

1 *The removal of all surface dust.*
2 *The keeping clean and bright of all polished surfaces, i.e. polished wood floors, furniture, windows, mirrors, etc.*
3 *The general tidying-up of all the rooms in daily use.*

In addition, there was a correct sequence in which these tasks should be carried out:

1 *Collect all apparatus and equipment.*
2 *Remove all dust and waste water:*
   (a) Clean the fire-place and re-lay the fire.
   (b) Clean the washstand or fitted hand-basin.
   (c) Sweep the floor.
   (d) Dust all ledges as high as the upstretched arm can reach, and dust all furniture and ornaments.
   NOTE: *Beds should be made before starting to sweep the floor.*
3 *Rub up all bright surfaces, the polished floor last of all.*
4 *Give the room a general tidying.*
5 *If the cleaning equipment is not to be used for other rooms, it can then be put tidily away.*

From A STUDENT'S HANDBOOK OF HOUSEWIFERY by MISS A.M. KAYE, 1940

Man's work lasts till set of sun
A woman's work is never done.

TRADITIONAL SAYING

THE WEEKLY ROUTINE

"We give the following routine of the work of an imaginary small house, where there would be one or two servants only to wait upon and serve a family of four or six persons.

MONDAY
The home washing.

TUESDAY
Sweeping and cleaning of servants' bedroom or one or two other rooms, and stairs cleaned down to lower floor.

WEDNESDAY
The sweeping and cleaning of best bedroom, and windows.

THURSDAY
Cleaning and turning out of cupboards, and cleaning of passages and remaining stairs.

FRIDAY
Sweeping and cleaning of drawing room, and cleaning of silver.

SATURDAY
Sweeping and cleaning of dining room and kitchen, tins, coppers, etc.

Besides these daily tasks mentioned, must be reckoned the bed-making, the dusting, the cooking and washing-up, and all the hundred and one things that have to be accomplished in the smallest of households…"

From MRS BEETON'S COOKERY BOOK, 1914

EARLY TO RISE

"We are all creatures of example, servants and children being no exception to the rule, and it seldom happens that a late mistress does not make a late household...

There is no work like morning work, particularly household tasks, and those we take up early in the day, when fresh from a night's rest and a good breakfast, are 'trifles light as air' in comparison with the same dragged or hurried through later when there is not time for their proper performance."

From MRS BEETON'S COOKERY BOOK, 1914

WASHDAY

Before the advent of washing machines and tumble dryers to make the washing and drying of clothes a relatively painless affair, washing had to be done by hand. Monday was the day traditionally set aside for this laborious activity.

They that wash on Monday
Have all the week to dry;
They that wash on Tuesday
Are not so much awry;
They that wash on Wednesday
Are not so much to blame;
They that wash on Thursday
Wash for very shame;
They that wash on Friday
Wash in sorry need;
They that wash on Saturday
Are lazy sluts indeed.

TRADITIONAL RHYME

A CLEAN FLOOR

For centuries, women cleaned floors – usually made of mud or stone – by sweeping them, and then strewed them with sweet-smelling herbs in place of carpets. Queen Elizabeth I of England is said to have favored meadowsweet for this purpose because of its fresh, delicate perfume.

HOUSEWIFE AS DAIRYMAID

"The woman must sit on the near side of the Cow, and she must gently at the first handle and stretch her Dugs, and moisten them with Milk, that they may yield out the Milk the better, and with less pain. She shall not settle herself to Milk, nor fix her Pail firm to the ground, till she see the Cow stand sure and firm, but be ready upon any motion of the Cow to save her Pail from overturning. She shall then milk the Cow boldly, and not leave stretching or straining of her teats, till not one drop of Milk more will come from them: for the worst point of Housewifery that can be is to leave a Cow half milked… it is the only way to make a Cow dry, and utterly unprofitable for the Dairy. She shall do nothing rashly or suddenly about the Cow, which may frighten or amaze her; but as she came gently, so with all gentleness she shall depart."

From THE ENGLISH HOUSEWIFE, 1683

MODERN CONVENIENCES

"A gas cooker is so clean and convenient to work with that the mistress of the house need not hesitate to use it herself if her servants are out, or for the purpose of trying some new dish. The gas cooker saves time, labour and expense."

BRITISH COMMERCIAL GAS ASSOCIATION ADVERTISEMENT, 1914

THE WAY TO A MAN'S HEART

"The well fed man is a happy man – and a very easily 'managed' one too. And since we women know that to maintain harmony every man, however clever, however efficient, however charming, must be 'managed', let us feed him well first and manage him afterwards."

From FEED THE BRUTE by MARJORIE SWIFT, 1925

AN AMPLE TABLE

As mistress of the house, part of the housewife's role extended to entertaining. If a dinner party was to be successful, certain requirements had to be observed. The guests should, for example, have ample room at table to enjoy their meal in comfort. Writing on this subject, Mrs. Isabella Beeton, the celebrated English authority on cookery and home management, advised that the hostess should allow a minimum of 24 inches per person, warning that "there is no greater misery than to be crowded."

AVOIDING HOUSEWORK

The Japanese courtesan Sei Shonagon gave some simple advice on dealing with housework and home maintenance – don't do it:

"When a woman lives alone, her house should be extremely dilapidated, the mud wall should be falling to pieces, and if there is a pond, it should be overgrown with water-plants."

From THE PILLOW BOOK OF SEI SHONAGON, TENTH CENTURY

LADIES OF LEISURE

Those fortunate women who were not slaves to the chores of housework were faced with the problem of whiling away the vacant hours:

"The intention of your being taught needlework, knitting and such like is not on account of the intrinsic value of all you can do with your hands, which is trifling, but to enable you to fill up, in a tolerably agreeable way, some of the many solitary hours you must necessarily pass at home."

DR. GREGORY, 1770

Curly locks, Curly locks,
Wilt thou be mine?
Thou shalt not wash dishes
Nor yet feed the swine;
But sit on a cushion
And sew a fine seam,
And feed upon strawberries,
Sugar and cream.

TRADITIONAL RHYME

CHAPTER FIVE
WORKING WOMEN

"Creative minds have always been known to survive any kind of bad training."

ANNA FREUD (1895-1982)

WOMEN HAVE WORKED SINCE THE DAWN OF TIME, MAKING PRACTICAL CONTRIBUTIONS, BOTH PAID AND UNPAID, TO THE BUSINESS OF LIVING. TODAY, WOMEN'S ACHIEVEMENTS SHINE FORTH FROM EVERY SPHERE, AND YET FURTHER ENCOURAGEMENT IS STILL NEEDED. THESE FACTS, STORIES, AND ANECDOTES ABOUT WORKING WOMEN THROUGHOUT THE AGES SHOULD PROVE INSPIRING TO EVERY WOMAN WHO WANTS TO FORGE AHEAD IN THE MODERN WORLD.

CAREER CHOICES

There are few jobs that women cannot do or, historically, have not done. Women in the ancient world enjoyed a wide range of career options – ironically, over the centuries these became increasingly limited by ideas of "suitability." It is only now, in the twentieth century, that women have won back freedoms of choice that were available centuries ago.

IN THE STONE AGE

Stone Age women led short, active lives, often dying by the time they were twenty. Their working day encompassed both the basic tasks necessary for human survival and activities that mark the dawning of creativity. Much of the work they did is still primarily associated with women today. A Stone Age woman's working week would have included:

- Fashioning clothes from animal skins
- Making pots and vessels from clay and animal skins
- Weaving baskets
- Making jewelry
- Making tools to facilitate all these crafts
- Gathering roots, berries, and other edible plant food
- Cooking
- Caring for children
- Making shelters.

IN ANCIENT EGYPT

The list of occupations from which an ancient Egyptian woman could choose included:

- Midwife
- Merchant
- Builder (of pyramids)
- Property owner
- Farmer
- Weaver
- Potter
- Temple dancer
- Musician
- Artist
- Poet
- Priestess
- Earthly representative of a goddess (as many a powerful Egyptian queen believed herself to be).

IN ANCIENT ROME

In the Roman world, women's career options included:

- Doctor
- Librarian
- Hairdresser
- Dressmaker
- Laundress
- Musician
- Dancer
- Prostitute
- Vestal Virgin
- Sibyl and seer.

IN ANCIENT GREECE

In first-century Greece, there were three thousand women working as sought-after musicians and singers, a career which continued to provide women with a creative outlet and handsome income for centuries.

In Lydia, now part of modern Greece, women worked as stone-masons. They were not slaves, but chose the work themselves.

A LADYLIKE OCCUPATION

"I, a woman, have dropped the symbols of my sex,
Yarn, shuttle, basket, thread."
OLIMPIA MORATA (1526-55)

The idea of what constitutes an acceptable occupation for a woman has undergone many changes. Jobs involving heavy physical labor, exposure to rough language and behavior, decision making, and long hours have all, at one time or another, been considered unsuitable. However, this has not deterred women, either out of necessity or personal desire, from enduring such conditions – and in many instances, they have triumphed over them.

A THREAT TO MORALITY

"I wonder when we shall come to the conclusion that the work of a barmaid is derogatory to girls, and unite in trying to get that way of earning a living closed to them. Personally I think, however scarce work may be, that a calling which exposes a girl to the sight and hearing of what goes on amongst frequenters of public houses cannot fail in ninety-nine out of a hundred cases to have a very bad moral influence."
From HOME NOTES MAGAZINE, 1894

BAD LANGUAGE

"I hear that the introduction of lady clerks at the Bank of England at first caused a little friction. One lady had to be visited by pains and penalties for insubordination to a superior, and it is actually said that she so far forgot herself as to make use of the expression 'An old frump!'"

From HOME NOTES MAGAZINE, 1894

A LITTLE RESPECT

Dorothea Woodward Fisher was born in the year the above opinions were voiced. The writer would hardly have approved of Dorothea's career choice, since the aptly named Mrs. Fisher ran one of the largest fleets of barges on the River Thames in London.

She started out in business with her husband, and continued to run it after his death until she was seventy-eight. She dressed for work in an original way, favoring a well-cut tailored suit, the choice of many women executives, but enlivening it with colorful accessories – a live parrot on one shoulder, a monocle in one eye, and an ever-present cigarette. She said of her work:

"I reckon a woman has to work for respect. I never met any prejudice on the river. But I have a gruff voice and I can be as tough as any man."

THE OLDEST PROFESSION

Women are credited with being the first to grow crops from seed and to tend domestic animals, working on the land in what is probably the oldest profession of all. Historically, the more affluent women, often widows, ran their own farms successfully – a literary example being Bathsheba in Thomas Hardy's *Far From the Madding Crowd*, who must have been drawn at least in part from real life.

On a more humble level, women farm laborers belied the notion that the female sex were too delicate to dirty their hands with physical work, as this official report, published in Britain in 1867, shows:

"The work of two women is usually required for every 75 acres of the light land, and a larger proportion for that which is heavier... Their labour consists in the various operations of cleaning the land, picking stones, weeds etc., turnip hoeing, hay making and harvest work, rooting and shawing, that is cleaning turnips, barn work with the thrashing and winnowing machines, filling dung carts, turning dung heaps, spreading the dung and sowing artificial manure, turnip cutting in the winter for sheep etc. and occasionally driving carts or harrowing. In some instances forking, pitching and loading hay or corn, though when such is the case two women are put to the work for one man... The Northumbrian women who do these kinds of labour are physically such a splendid race; their strength is such that they can vie with the men in carrying sacks of corn, and there seems to be no work which affects them injuriously, however hard it may appear to be."

DOMESTIC SERVICE

For those women without the benefits of a wealthy background, entering domestic service was one of the few ways they could earn a living. A typical day for a maidservant began at five in the morning and ended at midnight. Most young women worked for an average of ten years, while saving up to get married. Those who remained single stayed in service and saved up for their old age, as there were no pensions.

Wages were far from handsome. In the 1780s, for example, British kitchen maids were paid £2 per half year, plus an additional allowance for purchasing tea.

The servant who at table waits,
Should have a ready eye;
For 'tis not all, to hand to plates
And silently stand by.

The table neatly to set out,
As it before was planned;
To move with noiseless step about,
to serve with gentle hand.

To cast a look from side to side,
And read in every face
If any want is unsupplied,
Or unfill'd any space.

To have whatever's call'd for near;
To speak no useless word;
To hear, yet never seem to hear,
What passes at the board;

These, of a clever parlour maid,
The special duties are;
And she who hopes to be well-paid,
Must make them all her care.

From LESSONS ON INDUSTRIAL EDUCATION FOR THE USE OF FEMALE SCHOOLS by A LADY, 1849

FACTORY GIRLS

Women who worked in factories began at a very tender age. Sophia Cockin, interviewed for an official report in 1865, described her experience in the Sheffield cutlery trade, in the north of England:

"I began cutting work at six years old. They lifted me on a stool to reach my work, as I was not big enough to get up myself. My lass, now dead, began cutting when two weeks turned six years old. Bless you! You'll find little ones at it up and down now, some, I daresay, nearly as young as I was."

At the end of a long day, however, the "factory girls" managed to put thoughts of work behind them:

"There is no mistaking her in the streets. The long day's silence is made up for the moment she is free, by loud and boisterous laughter and a flow of language peculiar to her and her alone. No pavement ever seems quite wide enough for her requirements, as she strolls along from side to side, arm in arm with two kindred spirits."
LETTICE BELL (NINETEENTH CENTURY)

MINEWORKERS

Isabel Hogg, fifty-three years old at the time of her interview by the Children's Employment Commission (1842), was a coal bearer in Victorian England. She had been married for thirty-seven years, for it was common practice to marry early. Although miscarriage was a frequent result of working while pregnant, Isabel had four adult daughters who also worked in the mines, carrying coals on their backs. Stoical and extremely strong, Isabel dreamed of a better world for her daughters and grand-daughters. She told her interviewers:

"Women people here don't mind work, but they object to horse-work; and that she [Queen Victoria] would have the blessings of all the Scotch coal-women if she would get them out of the pits, and send them to other labour."

A ROYAL PROFESSION

At the opposite end of the social spectrum, another occupation open to women – and one almost as old as that of working on the land – was the job of queen. Originally, "queen" simply meant a woman who owned land, which in ancient societies she did as a matter of course, sometimes exclusively. Over time, the word came to mean a powerful female figurehead.

"Women have been called queens for a long time, but the kingdom given them isn't worth ruling."
LOUISA MAY ALCOTT (1832-88)

QUALITIES OF A QUEEN

Being a queen is a job which a woman is generally born to, and in which she exercises the same power as any king. But throughout history, many women have poisoned, schemed, manipulated, and fought for this position. Some of them, like Catherine the Great, Empress of Russia, succeeded magnificently. Others, like Roxelana, a harem girl who became a formidable power behind the throne in the Ottoman Empire, came to mysterious or violent ends. In willpower and energy, however, such women were more than equal to their masculine counterparts and provide an inspiring example for others of their sex.

HARD WORK

Catherine the Great (1729-96) possessed quite amazing energy, routinely working fifteen hours a day at her job – ruling Russia. Her self-imposed duties included:

- Rewriting the law
- Reorganizing the army
- Reorganizing the navy
- Writing letters to famous intellectuals such as Voltaire and Diderot
- Educating Russian women
- Training new officials to administer the outposts of her empire.

In her spare time, she wrote plays and fables for her own amusement and to entertain her many friends. She also conducted an exotic, romantic, and busy love life; "My heart hates to be a single hour without love," she maintained.

CARE AND LOVE

Queen Elizabeth I of England (1533-1603) – whose reign marked one of the most glorious periods in English history – also evinced great energy, and unswerving commitment to her role in life:

"There will never Queen sit in my seat with more zeal to my country, care to my subjects, and that will sooner with willingness venture her life for your good and safety, than myself. For it is my desire to live nor reign no longer than my life and reign shall be for your good. And though you have had and may have many princes more mighty and wise sitting in this seat, yet you never had nor shall have any that will be more careful and loving."
QUEEN ELIZABETH I OF ENGLAND, 1601

COMPASSION

Compared with some other monarchs, one queen at least – the exotically named Ranavalona of Madagascar – had uncharacteristically high ethical standards:

"In several ways Queen Ranavalona might put to shame her more civilized sisters. She will never tolerate any overt acts of cruelty, and has the greatest reluctance to sign execution warrants."
From HOME NOTES MAGAZINE, 1894

A LITTLE LEARNING

"If women are expected to do the same work as men, we must teach them the same things."
PLATO (c.427-c.347 B.C.)

Education opens the door to career opportunities that might not be otherwise accessible. Historically, the question of education for ordinary people – of both sexes – has been hedged about with restrictions. For knowledge is power, and in trying to claim such power women and men have had to fight very hard.

The idea of education for women has been plagued with its own particular difficulties. Less than a century ago, it was believed that women had less capacity for thinking because their brains weighed less than a man's. If a woman did show an aptitude for learning, she was thought to have sacrificed her femininity on the altar of academic achievement.

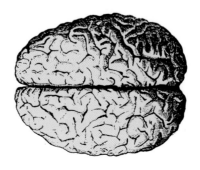

RIVALS

The linguist, scholar, author, and governess Elizabeth Elstob (1683-1756) questioned, with feigned innocence, whether the resistance to educating women might not be due to just a touch of jealous and unseemly rivalry:

"For first, I know it will be said, What has a woman to do with learning? This I have known urged by some men, with an envy unbecoming that greatness of soul, which is said to dignify their sex."

A BETTER WAY

Frances Mary Buss (1827-94) – pioneering founder and headmistress, for more than forty years, of a well-known North London girls' school – was a ceaseless champion of education for women:

"As I have grown older, the terrible sufferings of women of my own class, for want of good elementary training, have more than ever intensified my earnest desire to lighten…the misery of women brought up 'to be married and taken care of', and left alone in the world destitute."

PHILOSOPHICAL WOMEN

In the third century A.D., two women, dressed as men, studied at the philosopher Plato's famous Academy. We do not know their names, but there were a number of distinguished female philosophers in ancient times – three of them so celebrated that their names have come down to us across the ages:

- Hipparchia, who lived in Athens during the third-century B.C., asserted that she was proud to have "used the time I would have wasted on weaving for my education."
- Beruriah lived in Jerusalem in the second century A.D. and was married to a Rabbi Meir. A number of her observations are recorded in the Talmud, each beginning "Rightly did Beruriah say…"
- Hypatia lived in Alexandria, now part of modern Egypt, between the fourth and fifth centuries A.D. She was an inventor, popular teacher, philosopher, mathematician, and astronomer.

FOOD FOR THOUGHT

"To have no food for our heads, no food for our hearts, no food for our activity, is that nothing? If we have no food for the body, how do we cry out, how all the world hears to it, how all the newspapers talk of it, with a paragraph headed in great capital letters, 'Death from Starvation!' But suppose one were to put a paragraph in THE TIMES, 'Death of Thought from Starvation', or 'Death of Moral Activity from Starvation', how people would stare, how they would laugh and wonder!"

FLORENCE NIGHTINGALE (1820-1910)

WRITERS AND POETS

Women who were able to read and write were, for centuries, members of a privileged elite; and among them were some exceptionally gifted creative writers. Since writing was at least semi-respectable, it was one way a woman could earn her living without attracting too much censure. As such, it became not only a creative activity but a means of basic survival for those educated women who fell upon hard times.

FIT FOR A GODDESS

Of the work of the most ancient women writers, only fragments have survived. Sappho of Lesbos, for example, wrote nine books of poetry, yet only one poem has come down to us intact. Of the rest, no more than tantalizing pieces survive. She was born around 630 B.C. on the Greek island of Lesbos, where she ran a kind of religious school for women, dedicated to the goddess of love and art, Aphrodite. She is renowned for her tender love poetry, which remains poignantly evocative. Infamous as a lover of women, she did, in fact, marry and have a daughter, Cleis, whom she compared to "golden flowers."

> *The isles of Greece, the isles of Greece!*
> *Where burning Sappho loved and sung…*
> From DON JUAN by LORD BYRON (1788-1824)

WRITING FOR MONEY

Fanny Trollope (1780-1863), mother of the novelist Anthony Trollope, supported her family by her writing. Her output was prodigious, totalling 114 volumes. But none of these did as well as her runaway bestseller *The Domestic Manners of the Americans*, in which she described her experiences of three years in America. Her son paid touching tribute to her: "Of all people I have known she was the most joyous or, at any rate, the most capable of joy."

FOR RICHER, FOR POORER

Eliza Acton, a talented Victorian cookery writer and poet, made an ironic comment on the impecunious state of many writers, compared with the affluence of their publishers, in her book *Modern Cookery* (1845). In it she included two conspicuously literary recipes. Of "The Publisher's Pudding," she observed: "This pudding can scarcely be made *too* rich." And it is indeed a rich concoction, containing, among other ingredients, lashings of cream, brandy, almonds, and macaroons. In stark and mischievous contrast was her recipe for "The Poor Author's Pudding" – a simple bread-and-butter pudding made with milk.

WHAT'S IN A NAME?

Women writers frequently had to employ subterfuge in order to achieve publication of their work. Charlotte Brontë, for example, began her career as a published novelist under the male pen-name Currer Bell. (Her publishers were astonished when she revealed herself as a woman.) And who has ever heard of Mary Ann Evans – the real name of the great Victorian novelist and poet George Eliot?

To be a woman and a writer
Is double mischief, for
The world will slight her
Who slights 'the servile house', and who would rather
Make odes than beds.

DILYS LAING (1906-60)

THE REWARDS OF DISCIPLINE

The novelist George Sand (1804-76) was enviably dis-
ciplined in her work and developed a strict routine of
writing for eight hours every day. In this way she was
able to produce two or three books a year, despite
the passionate vicissitudes of her colorful domestic
life. One of her lovers, the writer Alfred de Musset,
ruefully observed:

*"I had worked all day, and by the evening had pro-
duced ten lines and drunk a bottle of brandy. She, on
the other hand, had polished off a litre of milk and
written half a volume."*

ARTISTS

There have been countless women artists, many of them
anonymous, whose work was mistakenly attributed to
men in less enlightened times.

PROPRIETY

Like writing, for centuries the visual arts hovered on the brink of respectability. There were numerous women court painters, for instance, because it was thought more suitable for portraits of the young, unmarried women at court to be painted by female artists.

Portraiture also made it possible for the British painter Catherine Read to practice her art. She was the first unmarried female art student to study abroad, first in Paris and then in Rome, and by the 1770s had become the most popular portrait painter of her time. She restricted herself to this mode of expression because, as someone who knew her well wrote, her sex made it "impossible for her to attend public academies or even design or draw from nature."

"An artist's life of freedom beckoned to me with all its magic; with its troubles, but with its rewarding, delightful undertakings as well."
CAROLINE LUISE SEIDLER, PAINTER TO THE COURT OF SAXONY, 1837

IMPROPRIETY

The charismatic Suzanne Valadon (1869-1938), an outstanding artist and mother of the painter Maurice Utrillo, threw the rulebook away and simply refused to allow convention to stifle her outrageous free spirit. At forty-three, she left her husband for a man twenty-one years her junior, and lived and painted in Paris with her lover. Their relationship lasted for more than twenty years, during which time she created some of her most arresting pictures.

"I am a painter, I have earned my living honestly. My private life is nobody's concern. I have only to thank God for the protection he has always granted me by giving me a guardian angel in my friend [her lover]."
ROSA BONHEUR (1822-99)

ART AND DOMESTICITY

Women artists have had to combine art with domesticity to a much greater degree than their male counterparts. Some have found this easier to cope with than others.

The artist Stella Bowen fell deeply in love with the writer Ford Madox Ford in 1918. Her eight-year relationship with him subsumed her creative energy, although she was "happy and absorbed" until he became repeatedly unfaithful, whereupon she left him. She wrote of the difficulties that professional women had to contend with – and still face today:

"A man writer or painter always managed to get some woman to look after him and make his life easy, and since female devotion, in England anyhow, is a glut on the market, this is not difficult. A professional woman, however, seldom gets this cushioning, unless she can pay money for it."

In contrast, the distinguished British abstract sculptor, Barbara Hepworth (1903-75), who had triplets by fellow artist Ben Nicholson, seems to have positively reveled in the challenge of combining motherhood and art. Of conditions in her studio, she said:

"My studio was a jumble of children, rocks, sculptures, trees, importunate flowers and washing."

HEALTHCARE

A great singer must always take care of her throat. Jenny Lind, known as "the Swedish Nightingale," who was one of the most famous sopranos of all time, favored a soothing soup to lubricate her vocal cords. This recipe was part of her own culinary repertoire:

"Wash a quarter of a pound of the best pearl sago until the water poured from it is clear; stew it quite tender and very thick in water or thick broth: then mix gradually with it a pint of good boiling cream, and the yolks of four fresh eggs, and mingle the whole carefully with two quarts of strong veal or beef stock, which should always be kept ready boiling. Send the soup immediately to table."

TIPS FOR THE TOP

"A woman must have money and a room of her own."
VIRGINIA WOOLF, NOVELIST AND CRITIC (1882-1941)

"Women who set a low value on themselves make life hard for other women."
NELLIE L. McCLUNG, WRITER (1873-1951)

"Life is to be lived. If you have to support yourself, you had bloody well better find some way that is going to be interesting. And you don't do that by sitting around wondering about yourself."
KATHARINE HEPBURN, FILM STAR (b. 1909)

"I do not know anyone who has got to the top without hard work. That is the recipe. It will not always get you to the top, but should get you pretty near."
MARGARET THATCHER, BRITISH PRIME MINISTER 1979-90

"To be successful, the first thing to do is fall in love with your work."
SISTER MARY LAURETTA, CATHOLIC NUN

AND FINALLY…

The qualities that every woman needs if she wants to succeed in her chosen path – courage, determination, vision, and hope – are perfectly expressed in this stirring song sung by the women chain-makers of Cradley Heath, England, when they went on strike in 1910 to win a better life for themselves:

Rouse, ye women, long enduring,
Beat no iron, blow no bellows
Till ye win the fight, ensuring
Pay that is your due.

CHORUS
Through years uncomplaining,
Hope and strength are waning,
Your industry
A beggar's fee,
And meagre fare was gaining.
Now a Trade Board is created,
See your pain and dearth abated,
And the Sweater's wiles checkmated
Parliament's decree!

Rouse, ye women, rouse, around you
Towns and Cities cry, "God speed you,"
Rouse, shake off the fears that bound you
Women, rouse. Be true.

At length the light is breaking,
The Sweater's throne is shaking,
Oh, do your part,
With all your heart,
A sweeter world in making!
Stand together, strong and splendid,
In your Union till you've ended
Tyranny, and with toil blended
Beauty, Joy and Art.

CHAPTER SIX

WILD, WILD WOMEN

Cigarettes and whisky and wild, wild women
They'll drive you crazy, they'll drive you insane...
OLD SONG

IN EVERY CENTURY, IN EVERY CULTURE, THERE HAVE BEEN WILD
WOMEN. LONG AGO THEY WERE PERSONIFIED BY POWERFUL
GODDESS FIGURES IN WHOM THE QUALITIES OF LOVE AND
VENGEANCE MINGLED INEXTRICABLY. WILD WOMEN HAVE KEPT
ALIVE THIS TIMELESS ARCHETYPE BY REFUSING TO CONFORM,
CAPITULATE, OR SURRENDER
THEIR INDIVIDUALITY.

LOVE OF LIFE

"I like living. I have sometimes been wildly, despairingly, acutely miserable, racked with sorrow, but through it all I still know quite certainly that just to be alive is a grand thing."
AGATHA CHRISTIE (1891-1976)

THE STORY OF ARTEMIS

The great goddess Artemis could be said to typify the essence of independent womanhood. As a little girl, she begged Zeus, her father, for a bow and arrows to hunt with, a knee-length tunic to wear so she could run free, and all the mountains and forests for her domain. But, above all, she pleaded that she should be allowed to keep her girlhood liberty for ever. Her wishes were granted, and she became known as "Mistress of Animals." Her splendid temple at Ephesus (now in Turkey) was one of the Seven Wonders of the World.

"Every woman is a rebel, and usually in wild revolt against herself."
OSCAR WILDE (1856-1900)

WARRIOR WOMEN

Artemis was the goddess of the Amazons – the battle-fit, women warriors, whose legendary armies were said to be invincible. Their beautiful, vengeful ghosts had to be placated, and they were believed to sacrifice to Artemis any men who trespassed on their land. Above all, they were superb horsewomen, credited with being the first to tame horses. Their passion for exercise lived on in the Greek culture of Sparta, where girls and boys trained and wrestled together as a matter of course.

For centuries, the Amazons were regarded as pure myth, an unlikely creation of the ancient Greek imagination. But it seems they did exist, and their battling spirit has survived to inspire modern women by expanding our notions of femininity.

*"You were once wild here.
Don't let them tame you!"*
ISADORA DUNCAN (1878-1927)

TOMBOYS

Spartan girls were among the first tomboys – a type, it seems, that has always invited reproach:

"Wish as you might, a Spartan girl never could be virtuous. They gad abroad with young men with naked thighs, and with clothes discarded, they race with 'em, wrestle with 'em. Intolerable!"
From ANDROMACHE by EURIPIDES (484-406 B.C.)

FEMALE KNIGHTS

"It is better to die on your feet than to live on your knees."
DOLORES IBARRURI, KNOWN AS LA PASIONARA (1895-1989)

Founded by Napoleon I in 1804, the Legion of Honor awards its order of merit to men and women. In the first six years of its existence, three women warriors were awarded its highest honor, the title of Knight of the Legion of Honor, while several others were awarded the Cross for outstanding bravery. Their stories, and indeed the realization of their very existence, are all the more inspiring for they are set in the nineteenth century – a period that was particularly oppressive for women.

THE PRETTY SERGEANT

Virginie Ghesquire – known as *La Jolie Sergeant* (the pretty sergeant) – successfully took the place of her delicate brother, who could not fulfill his military duties, and managed to pass herself off as a man until she was wounded. She was knighted for her devotion to her brother and her country.

THE GLORY OF THE EMPIRE

Marie Schellinck fought at the battles of Jeneappes, Austerlitz, and Jena. Her bravery was such that Napoleon took the cross off his own breast to decorate her, saying, "Madame, I bestow on you a pension of seven hundred francs, and I make you a Knight of the Legion of Honor. Receive from my hands the Star of Bravery, which was so nobly acquired." Turning to his officers, he said, "Bow respectfully before this woman, for she is one of the glories of my Empire."

"The only courage that matters is the kind that gets you from one minute to the next."
MIGNON McLAUGHLIN

AROUND THE WORLD

When her husband abandoned her and her baby died, Hannah Snell (1728-92) refused to give in. Disguised as a young man, she became both a soldier and, subsequently, an assistant steward and cook in the navy. In a fruitless attempt to find her absent husband, she sailed as far as India, where she was severely wounded in battle. But Hannah was a survivor. Learning that her husband was dead, she abandoned her military career and returned to London to run a pub aptly named "The Female Warrior."

ASSERTING HER RIGHTS

Orphaned Mary Ann Talbot became mistress to a Captain Bowen when she was about fourteen years old. Disguised as his page, she accompanied him on board a ship bound for Valenciennes, where her dubious protector was killed in action. She promptly joined the British navy as a cabin boy, and was wounded in the Battle of Brest. Still in disguise, she returned to London, and went to claim her pension and prize money. She was told to come back later, whereupon she lost her temper in spectacular fashion. As a result, she ended up in front of an astounded magistrate – who ordered that a subscription be raised to pay her until her pension came through.

"A woman is seldom roused to great and courageous exertion but when something most dear to her is in immediate danger."
JOANNA BAILLIE (1762-1851)

A QUEEN'S REVENGE

Boudicca, Queen of the Iceni, one of the tribes of ancient Britain, was said to be very tall, with a mass of waist-length tawny hair, and a commanding voice. Betrayed by the Roman conquerors, who beat her and raped her daughters, she led her troops against them in a magnificent but doomed bid for revenge.

"I am not fighting for my kingdom and wealth now. I am fighting as an ordinary person for my lost freedom, my bruised body, and my outraged daughters."
From THE ANNALS OF IMPERIAL ROME by TACITUS (c.55-120 A.D.)

PIONEER SPIRITS

The nineteenth-century women pioneers of the American West had a good deal in common with the legendary Amazons of ancient Greece. These indomitable women forged a life for themselves and their families, farming, fighting, hunting, and surviving undaunted in the toughest conditions. Here are the views of one Wyoming woman, Elinore Pruitt Stewart, on the rewards of life as a rancher:

"To me, homesteading is the solution of all poverty's problems, but I realize that temperament has much to do with success in any undertaking and persons afraid of coyotes and work and loneliness had better let ranching alone. At the same time, any woman who can stand her own company, can see the beauty of the sunset, loves growing things, and is willing to put in as much time at careful labor as she does over the washtub, will certainly succeed; will have independence, plenty to eat all the time, and a home of her own in the end."
From LETTERS OF A WOMAN HOMESTEADER (LATE NINETEENTH CENTURY)

A CRAZY WOMAN

Calamity Jane, legendary figure of the Wild West, was many things: "champion swearer of the hills," friend of Wild Bill Hickok and Buffalo Bill, scout, gambler, gold prospector, midwife, cook, prostitute, and "heroine of a thousand thrilling adventures." As tough as old riding boots and as sentimental as any young girl, she often rode alone up into the hills on her beloved horse, Satan. She was unafraid of the Sioux, she said, because, "They think I'm a crazy woman and never molest me."

IN SEARCH OF ADVENTURE

"No pessimist ever discovered the secrets of the stars, or sailed to an uncharted land, or opened a new heaven to the human spirit."
HELEN KELLER (1880-1968)

"Curiosity is one of the forms of feminine bravery."
VICTOR HUGO (1802-83)

Female explorers have, throughout history, traveled far and wide through conditions almost unimaginable to today's tourist. Whether driven by curiosity, necessity, or willfulness, their journeys remain an enduring record of feminine adventurousness. Such bold, unconventional women – like the redoubtable Lady Hester Stanhope, explorer, astrologer, and champion of the Bedouin tribes of Syria – were clearly not too concerned with others' opinions of them:

"I am contented with the violence of my own character; it draws a line for me between friends and enemies."
LADY HESTER STANHOPE (1776-1839)

ARAB HOSPITALITY

Lucie Duff Gordon (1821-69) spent seven years in Luxor in Egypt. She was trying to cure herself of consumption, and thought the hot, dry climate would benefit her. She became a beloved figure there, and wrote many letters to her family back in England vividly describing Egyptian life of the time. She was especially impressed by Arab hospitality, as exemplified by a chance invitation at Aswan in February, 1863:

"I had been strolling about in that most poetically melancholy spot, the granite quarry of old Egypt and burial-place of Muslim martyrs, and as I came homewards ... a party of merchants ... asked me to dinner, and, oh! how delicious it felt to sit on a mat among the camels and strange bales of goods and eat the hot tough bread, sour milk and dates, offered with such stately courtesy."

AN ACCIDENTAL EGYPTOLOGIST

Amelia Blandford Edwards (1831-92) became a respected Egyptologist quite by chance when her travel itinerary was changed on a whim. In her case, travel not only broadened the mind, but also resulted in an absorbing career. The subtle twist of fate that turned her footsteps towards Egypt led her to write *A Thousand Miles up the Nile* and to become joint founder of the Egypt Exploration Fund. When she died, she left enough money to establish the first chair of Egyptology in Britain. However, none of this could have been predicted at first, for, as she wrote:

"In simple truth we had drifted hither by accident, with no excuse of health, or business, or any serious object whatever; and had just taken refuge in Egypt as one might turn aside into the Burlington Arcade ... to get out of the rain."

BURLINGTON ARCADE An elegant mall of boutiques in Mayfair, a fashionable part of London.

DEALING WITH SNAKES

THE HOE TECHNIQUE

Alys Reece went to join her new husband in Kenya, Africa, in 1936. Her healthy fear of snakes resulted in an original method of dispatching them:

"The garden at Marsabit was very overgrown and there were any number of the kind of cobra that spit in your eye if you gave them a chance – and although I was terrified of them I knew that if I flicked them on to the grass with a special hoe that I'd sharpened they didn't have much chance. They were always racing for cover but with the very sharp hoe I could cut them in half before they got to it – and I became really quite vicious over them."

THE CLEFT STICK TECHNIQUE

Mary Kingsley, author of *Travels in West Africa* (1897), journeyed with four Africans into the forests of the Congo. She had an ironic sense of humor. Here is her advice on how to deal with snakes:

"Catching a snake in a cleft stick is perfectly simple. Only mind you have the proper kind of stick…and keep your attention on the snake's head, that's his business end…the tail, whisking and winding round your wrist, does not matter."

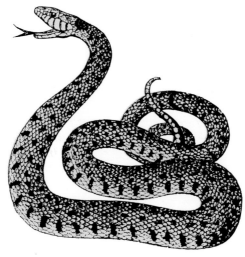

INDIAN TRANSPORT

The British in India have been the butt of many jokes, inspired numerous films and novels, and attracted considerable criticism – but the women who accompanied their husbands to India had to be adventurous and adaptable if they were to survive. Here is one woman's account of traveling during the cool season during the 1930s on an elephant that also carried the baby, the *ayah* (nurse), the cook, and the bearer:

"We used to all sit back very comfortably on one elephant. Sometimes the mahout [the driver] would have the baby sitting in front, on the elephant's head. When it got warm it would fill its trunk and spray us with water to keep us cool, and if we were eating an orange it would put its trunk back and take the orange and eat it."

MIDDLE-EASTERN MADNESS

Louisa Jebb, a Victorian woman who "once did crochet-work in drawing rooms," rode on horseback through Turkey and Iraq with one other woman. She threw off the shackles of convention in magnificent fashion when, encountering a group of men "dancing and stamping," she decided to join them:

"A feeling of wild rebellion took hold of me: I sprang into the circle. 'Make me mad!' I cried out. 'I want to be mad too!' The men seized me and on we went, on and on with the hopping and turning and stamping, and soon I too was a savage, a glorious free savage under the white moon."

ON THE WRONG SIDE OF THE LAW

"If... you can't be a good example, then you'll just have to be a horrible warning."
CATHERINE AIRD (b. 1930)

A woman's sense of limitation and frustration with her role is nothing new. Some women have expressed their pent-up energy in a life of crime. In Elizabethan times Mary Frith, known as Moll Cutpurse, was a notorious figure who dressed, fought, stole, and swore like a man. Her rationale for this colorful behavior was set out in her biography:

"She could not endure that sedentary life of sewing or stitching, a Sampler was as grievous as a Winding-sheet, her Needle, Bodkin and Thimble, she could not think on quietly, wishing them changed into Sword and Dagger for a bout at Cudgels..."
From THE LIFE AND DEATH OF MRS. MARY FIRTH, 1662

ADVICE FROM A PICKPOCKET

Jenny Diver (1705-40) used her considerable wit and creativity for nefarious ends. She came to what used to be called "a bad end," being hanged at Tyburn, London, in 1740, following her third arrest and trial. However, during her brief lifetime, her inventiveness was remarkable, as demonstrated by this, her most successful technique, described by the chaplain of Newgate Prison:

"Jenny had got two false arms made, and hands, by an ingenious artist, and dressing herself very genteely, like a citizen's wife, big with child with a pillow artfully fixed under her coats…and her arms fixed on, she hid her real ones under her petticoat, and the artificial ones came across her belly. Dressed in this condition, with one of her gang in the habit of a footman, she goes to the meeting house.

Now it was so ordered that our big-bellied lady was placed in a pew between two elderly ladies, who had both repeating watches by their side; she sat very quietly all the time of the service, but at the conclusion of the last prayer, the audience being standing she took both the ladies' watches off, and tipped them to one of her companions. Now the congregation breaking up, every body was in a hurry to get out, and the gang surrounded the ladies in order to make a greater crowd, and help Jenny off if she should be discovered."

HIGHWAY ROBBERY

Katherine Ferrers, says an old account, "took to highway robbery for the sheer love of adventure and the exercise of manly attributes." Born in 1634 and unhappily married at fourteen, Lady Ferrers sought her pleasures on the road. Disguised in a three-cornered hat, buckskin breeches, and cloak, she held up and robbed coaches. She died of wounds sustained in her last robbery, having ridden her black stallion like the wind to reach home, and the sanctuary of her secret room. A novel and, eventually, a film were based on her life.

A TOUCH OF BLACKMAIL

The sensational indiscretions of kiss-and-tell memoirs have been the last resort of many a spurned lover. An early exponent of this method of earning one's living was Harriette Wilson. When the Duke of Beaufort tried to bribe her not to continue an affair with his son, she was outraged and insulted. Her revenge was sweet. She wrote her memoirs, naming all her ex-lovers in four scandalous volumes.

On publication day, barriers had to be erected to control the crowds; and when Harriette threatened to publish more, her old flames clubbed together, in self-defence, to buy her off. This time she accepted the bribe – then married a Frenchman, and died a widow in 1846. The memorable opening lines to her first volume set the tone for what followed:

"I shall not say why and how I became, at the age of fifteen, the mistress of the Earl of Craven. Whether it was love, or the severity of my father, the depravity of my own heart, or the winning arts of the noble lord … does not now signify; or if it does, I am not in the humour to gratify curiosity in this matter."

WEARING THE TROUSERS

Women who dress in the same way as men have been viewed with consternation and horror in many quarters. As recently as the 1960s, women in trousers were banned from entering top-class restaurants and hotels. At a time when "women's lib" was surfacing, the furor seemed out of all proportion – after all, Eastern women had worn trouser-like garments for centuries. But the fuss was nothing new.

INDECENT APPAREL

In Berlin, in 1846, the poet Louise Aston so outraged the authorities by wearing trousers in public that they expelled her from the city for her sartorial crime.

WOMAN-ABOUT-TOWN

As might be expected, Parisians were more broad-minded than the citizens of some other countries, and took a more *laissez-faire* attitude to what people wore. One well-known Parisian, the writer George Sand, frequently dressed like a man so that she could move about freely; the conventional female attire of crinoline and delicate shoes, she said, made her feel like "a boat on ice." Her masculine disguise not only solved this problem very neatly, but also opened up hitherto undreamt-of possibilities for her, as a woman:

"With those steel-tipped heels I was solid on the sidewalk at last. I dashed back and forth across Paris and felt I was going around the world. My clothes were weatherproof too. I was out and about in all weathers, came home at all hours, was in the pit of all the theatres. Nobody heeded me, or suspected my disguise."
GEORGE SAND (1804-76)

RATIONAL DRESS

In 1849, the American social reformer Amelia Bloomer tried to introduce a more comfortable form of dress for women, so that heavy, restrictive corsets could be disposed of, along with layers of voluminous petticoats that hampered movement. Her proposed "rational dress" consisted of a short jacket and a skirt that came to just below the knee, worn over long trousers that were gathered at the ankle. For her efforts, she was mercilessly lampooned on both sides of the Atlantic – and *Punch,* a British magazine that tended to uphold the status quo, published this telling little rhyme:

> *"As the husband, shall the wife be;*
> *he will have to wear a gown*
> *If he does not quickly make her*
> *put her Bloomer short-coats down."*
>
> From PUNCH MAGAZINE, 1850

REVOLUTIONARY SPIRITS

"You've got to have something to eat and a little love in your life before you can hold still for any damn body's sermon on how to behave."
BILLIE HOLIDAY (1915-59)

On October 5th, 1789, eight thousand women marched to Versailles, the luxurious palace where Louis XVI and his queen, Marie Antoinette, lived in foolish disdain of their people's explosive mood. This "Day of the Market Women" erupted because no bread could be found in any of the markets in Paris. The women's fury found an outlet in wrecking the palace, and murdering the guards in the process. The event culminated in the royal family's flight from Versailles – the last journey they would take, save that to the guillotine.

"Qu'ils mangent de la brioche."
("Let them eat cake.")
Attributed to MARIE ANTOINETTE (1755-93)

VOTES FOR WOMEN

"Nothing has ever been got out of a British Parliament without something approaching a revolution."
EMMELINE PANKHURST (1858-1928)

Emmeline, Christabel, and Sylvia Pankhurst were the leading lights of the British Suffragette movement – the Women's Social and Political Union (WSPU). Their commitment and fearlessness led to many arrests, and eventually in 1928 to success, when the right of women to vote was finally granted. In pursuit of their cause, they were wild women indeed, and proud of it. As Emmeline Pankhurst said of herself, "I am what you call a hooligan!"

"I think they are too hysterical, they are too much disposed to be guided by feeling and not by cold reason, and … to refuse any kind of compromise. I do not think women are safe guides in government, they are very unsafe guides."
EARL OF HALSTEAD, 1907

FREEDOM FROM SLAVERY

Women's freedom became linked with the fierce campaign for the abolition of slavery in nineteenth-century America. At a women's rights convention in 1851 one woman, a former slave who was a passionate abolitionist, spoke movingly on behalf of all down-trodden women:

"That man over there says women need to be helped into carriages and lifted over ditches, and to have the best place everywhere. Nobody ever helps me into carriages or over puddles or gives me the best place – and ain't I a woman?

Look at this arm! I have ploughed and planted and gathered into barns and no man could head me – and ain't I a woman?

I could work as much and eat as much as a man – when I could get it – and bear the lash as well – and ain't I a woman?

I have borne thirteen children, and seen most of 'em sold off to slavery, and when I cried out with my mother's grief, none but Jesus heard me – and ain't I a woman?"

SOJOURNER TRUTH, 1851

BIBLIOGRAPHY & ACKNOWLEDGMENTS

**The author and publishers
gratefully acknowledge the following:**

Beauty for Free, Catherine Palmer, Jonathan Cape, 1981
Belly Dancing, Wendy Buonaventura, Virago, 1983
Discovering Women's History, Deirdre Beddoe, Pandora Press, 1983
Encyclopedia of Magic and Superstition, Octopus Books, 1974
Hints on Girl Guide Badges, Mrs. Janson Potts, Brown, Son & Ferguson, 1940
A History of Their Own, Vols 1 & 2, Bonnie S. Anderson & Judith P. Zinsser,
Penguin Books, 1990
Home Notes (magazines in bound volumes), Pearson, 1894-5
In Our Grandmother's Footsteps, Jennifer Clarke, Virago, 1984
Letters from Egypt, Lucie Duff Gordon, R. Brimley Johnson, 1902
Meditations for women who do too much, HarperCollins, 1992
Mrs Beeton's Cookery Book, Ward Lock, 1914
The Best of Eliza Acton, Eliza Acton, Penguin Books, 1974
The Book of Fortune-telling, ed. Madame Fabia, Daily Express Publications, 1935
The Goddess Within, Jennifer Barker Woolger & Roger J. Woolger,
Random Century, 1990
The Letters of Calamity Jane to her Daughter, Battle Axe Books, 1984
The Monstrous Regiment, Margaret Blackwood, André Deutsch, 1990
The Perpetual Almanack of Folklore, Charles Kightly, Thames & Hudson, 1987
The Pillow Book of Sei Shonagon, Penguin Books, 1971
The Quotable Woman, Running Press, 1991
The Twelve Olympians, Charles Seltman, Pan Books, 1952
The Woman's Encyclopedia of Myths and Secrets, Barbara G. Walker,
Harper & Row, 1983
The Women's History of the World, Rosalind Miles, Paladin Books, 1989
Woman as Healer, Jeanne Achterberg, Rider, 1991
Women in Antiquity, Charles Seltman, Pan Books, 1957

*"I've dreamt in my life dreams that have stayed with
me ever after, and changed my ideas; they've gone
through and through me, like wine through water,
and altered the colour of my mind."*

EMILY BRONTË (1818-48)